Day one, God said,
"Let there be light."
He gave us day
And gave us night.

The firmament
Appeared day two—
The clouds we see,
The sky so blue.

The third day of creation
God made dry land and the seas;
And also on that day, God made
The plants and all the trees.

The fourth day God made Saturn,
Venus, Mercury, and Mars;
For on this day God spoke and made
The sun and moon and stars.

The Lord God is so powerful,
Creating by His words,
That on day five He spoke and made
Sea creatures, fish, and birds.

Day six God made land animals,
And creeping creatures, too.
Then in His image God made man;
It's wonderful and true!

God looked and saw all He had made.
It was all good—the best!
The work was done. God set aside
The seventh day for rest.

The Lord God is most powerful!
We see what He can do.
The most amazing thing of all
Is He loves me and you!

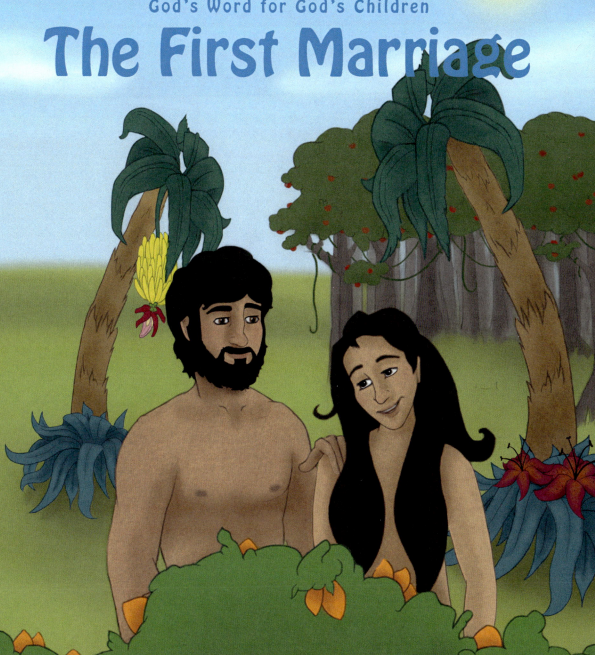

God's Word for God's Children
The First Marriage

And the Lord God caused a deep sleep to fall on Adam, and he slept; and He took one of his ribs, and closed up the flesh in its place. Then the rib which the Lord God had taken from man He made into a woman, and He brought her to the man. – Genesis 2:21-22

God, in the beginning,
Made the heavens and the earth.
He made the first man, Adam, too,
But not by normal birth.

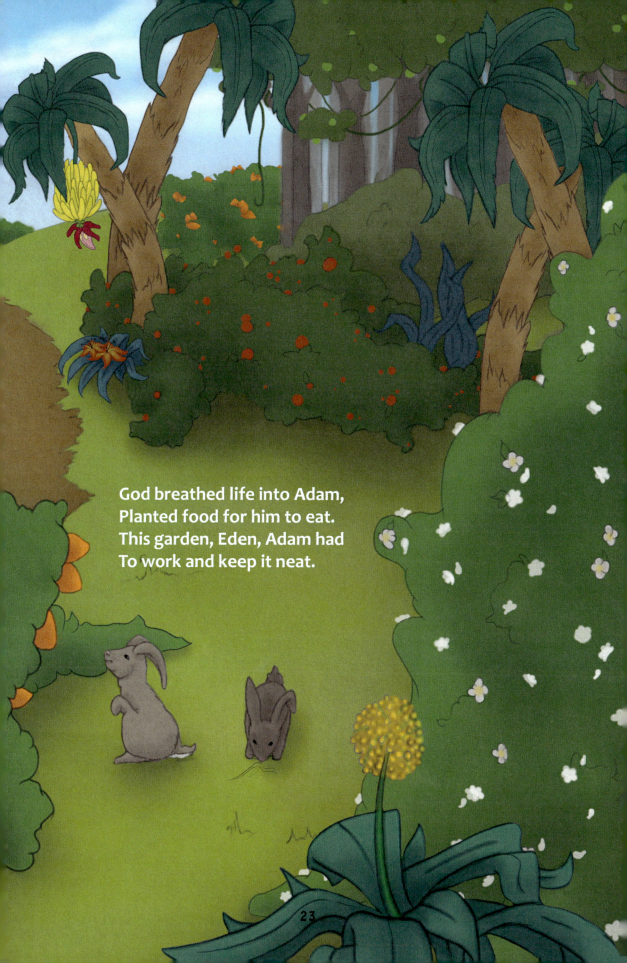

God breathed life into Adam,
Planted food for him to eat.
This garden, Eden, Adam had
To work and keep it neat.

The animals that run and walk and
Fly and jump and crawl,
God brought them all to Adam, and
Then Adam named them all.

God saw that Adam was alone—
No humans in his life.
He needed one to help him,
So God made for him a wife.

So God began our marriages—
A husband and a wife
Who love God and each other, and
Who stay that way for life.

God's Word for God's Children
The Garden of Eden

The Lord God planted a garden eastward in Eden, and there He put the man whom He had formed. And out of the ground the Lord God made every tree grow that is pleasant to the sight and good for food. The tree of life was also in the midst of the garden, and the tree of the knowledge of good and evil. – Genesis 2:8-9

The Garden of Eden was planted by God.
He had made it for Adam and Eve.
Now this is the story of how they first sinned,
And of why both of them had to leave.

Adam and Eve, they had never yet sinned,
And God gave them one simple command:
"From the tree of the knowledge of good and evil,
Don't eat, but enjoy all the rest of the land."

Satan appeared in the form of a snake,
And asked Eve, "Did God mean what He said?"
"God told us," said Eve, "If we eat of that tree,
We will certainly both end up dead."

"God was just saying that, Eve," said the snake.
"For surely that could not be true.
Here then is my theory of what will occur,
Of what eating that fruit now will do."

"Your eyes will be opened. You'll be just like God,
And you'll know good and evil," he said.
"Eve, listen to me. God made all those things up;
For I'm sure you will not end up dead."

They had sinned against God. They had done what was wrong.
They now realized that Satan had lied!
God was coming to see them, and they were afraid!
What could they do now? They would hide!

God called out to them, for He knew where they were.
He asked, "Why are you hiding, you two?
Did you disobey Me? Did you eat from the tree?
Did you do what I said not to do?"

"The woman You made for me gave me the fruit,"
Said Adam to God, "So I ate."
"The serpent deceived me," Eve said to the Lord.
"Satan told me the fruit would be great!"

God said to the serpent,
"Then cursed you shall be.
You will always eat dust,
Crawling on your belly."

To the woman, God said, "Here's your punishment, Eve;
For you disobeyed Me, it's true.
You will now have great pain giving birth to a child,
And your husband will rule over you."

To Adam, God said,
"You have sinned against Me.
For you listened to Eve,
And you ate from that tree."

"So now you must work by the sweat of your brow,
With thistles and thorns all around.
Created you were from the dust of the earth;
You will die and return to the ground."

The Lord made them clothes from some animal skins,
That Adam and Eve could now wear.
Then God sent them out of the garden He'd made.
They were never allowed back in there.

No matter what anyone else says to you,
You can trust in God's Word; it will always be true.
The Lord never lies, never leads us astray.
So follow God fully; it is the best way.

God tells about creation,
How everything began.
It's in the book of Genesis—
The history of man.

God's Word for God's Children

In the Beginning

Three Volumes in One
Genesis 1:1 – 3:24

Olin Edward James

Copyright © 2020
First edition published 2014
All rights reserved. No part of this book may be reproduced, stored in a retrieval system, or transmitted in any form or by any means – electronic, mechanical, photocopying, recording, or otherwise, without written permission from the publisher.

Scripture taken from the New King James Version®. Copyright © 1982 by Thomas Nelson. Used by permission. All rights reserved.

Illustrator: Jess Wadland
Author Family Photo: Esther Abel
Editor: Sharon Spencer

Printed in the United States of America
Aneko Press
www.anekopress.com
Aneko Press, Life Sentence Publishing, and our logos are trademarks of
Life Sentence Publishing, Inc.
203 E. Birch Street
P.O. Box 652
Abbotsford, WI 54405

JUVENILE NONFICTION / Religion / Bible Stories / Old Testament
Paperback ISBN: 978-1-62245-728-1
Available where books are sold.

10 9 8 7 6 5 4 3 2 1